Characteristics of Flight

Grades 4-6

Properties of Air
Paper Airplanes
Experiments
Invention Conference
How Planes Fly
Scientific Method
Famous Aviators
Activities/Puzzles
Answer Keys
Teacher Suggestions

About This Book

Explore the characteristics of flight and the properties of air through experimentation and investigation. This unit includes experiments, student activities, an invention conference, scientific method, famous aviators, types of aircraft, glossary of terms and answer keys.

D1533441

Written by: Paul and Clare Reid
Illustrated by: Paul and Clare Reid
Item #B1-101

Original Publication: 1999
Revision: 2000
©1999 P & C EDCON

Other Science Units

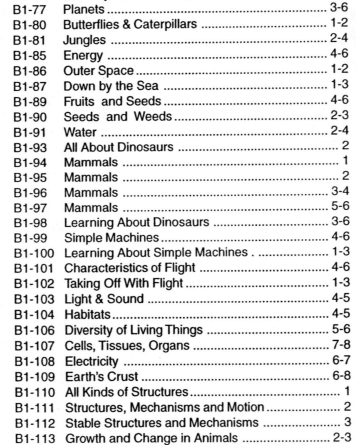

Published by:
S&S Learning Materials
15 Dairy Avenue
Napanee, Ontario
K7R 1M4

All rights reserved.
Printed in Canada.

Distributed in U.S.A. by:
T4T Learning Materials
5 Columba Drive, Suite 175
Niagara Falls, New York
14385

Table of Contents

Written by Paul and Clare Reid   Illustrated by Paul and Clare Reid

"We acknowledge the financial support of the Government of Canada through the Book Publishing Industry Development Program for our publishing activities."

ISBN 1-55035-610-0

 The students will demonstrate an awareness and understanding of the properties of air and principles of flight.

 The students will be able to recognize parts of an airplane and understand how they work together to allow an airplane to fly through the air.

 The students will understand and apply the scientific method when completing experiments.

 The students will be able to communicate their findings both orally and in written form.

 The students will have a basic knowledge of the forces exerted on an airplane during flight.

 The students will, through experimentation, demonstrate an understanding of the effect of forces acting upon one another.

 The students will be introduced to the invention process.

 The students will create their own inventions and participate in an Invention Conference.

 The students will apply a variety of strategies during group work to solve problems and record results.

 The students will recognize different types of aircraft.

 The students will develop an appreciation of the advances made in aviation through the study of aviators in history.

Teacher Suggestions

- Become familiar with the principles of flight.

- Experiment with the paper airplane templates before introducing them to the class.

- Use the experiments and activities provided in the "Properties of Air" section as an introduction to "Parts of a Plane" and "How Planes Fly".

- Encourage creativity when the students are designing their airplanes. Remind them to avoid using stickers, as these will affect the performance of their planes.

- Collect all materials required for the experiments and try the experiments before introducing them to the class.

- Encourage the students to ask their own questions and attempt to answer them through experimentation.

- Whenever possible, allow the students the opportunity to experience and learn through a "hands-on" approach.

- Select the activities which meet the needs of the individual students.

- You may choose to use the structured Scientific Method experiment sheets or create your own Learning Log or Journal for student response and evaluation.

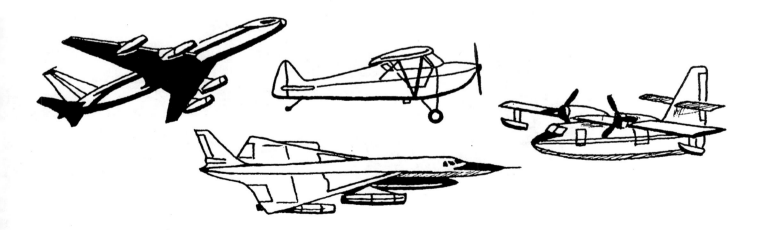

Bibliography

Boyd, Ian; <u>Super Stunts World's Best Paper Planes</u>;
Troll Books, ©1998

Caldecott, Barrie; <u>Kites</u>;
Franklin Watts, ©1990

Fredericks, Anthony; <u>Science Fair Handbook</u>;
Good Year Books, ©1990

Graham, Ian; <u>Transport How it Works</u>;
Sterling Publishing Company, ©1995

Jennings, Terry; <u>Planes Gliders Helicopters</u>;
Kingfisher Books, ©1993

Johnstone, Michael; <u>Look Inside Cross-Sections Planes</u>;
Scholastic Canada Ltd., ©1974

Macaulay, David; <u>The Way Things Work</u>;
Houghton Mifflin Company, ©1988

Rickard, Graham; <u>Helicopters</u>;
Wayland Publishers Ltd., ©1987

Scientific Method

The **"Scientific Method"** is a process which follows a logical progression to prove or disprove a given question. This is an excellent set of procedures for the beginning scientist to follow.

1 Consider a **Question** to investigate.

After asking a question, it is necessary to find resources before you can investigate. It is important to choose a question that is clear and one that the student is capable of answering.

> *Example*: Does air take up space?

2 **Predict** what will happen. (Hypothesis)

A hypothesis is an educated guess about the answer to a question being investigated. Insist that the students be thorough in their research and in the writing of their hypothesis.

> *Example*: I believe air does take up space.

3 Create a plan or **Procedure** to prove or disprove the hypothesis.

In devising a plan or set of procedures, the students must make a list of materials that will be required during their investigations. A numbered set of instructions must be written and strictly followed.

> *Example*: Place a piece of paper inside a glass and turn it upside down. Submerge the glass in a pail of water.

4 Record all of the **Observations** of the investigation.

It is very important that all observations be recorded in a data journal so that future investigations can benefit from those of the past. Results should be recorded in written and picture form.

Example: Water did not enter the glass and the paper remained dry.

5 Write a **Conclusion.**

A conclusion is a statement which answers the original question being asked. The conclusion must be supported by specific findings of the investigation. It is important to relate the experiment results to the hypothesis stated at the outset of the process.

Example:　The results of the experiment show that my original hypothesis was correct. Air does take up space.

It is very important that students be taught to accurately record results in their data journal on a daily basis. This journal can therefore be used by others to assist them or to continue the investigation. Any comments, observations or planned investigations in the future should be noted.

Scientific Method

The **"Scientific Method"** is a process which follows a logical progression to prove or disprove a given question. This is an excellent set of procedures for the beginning scientist to follow.

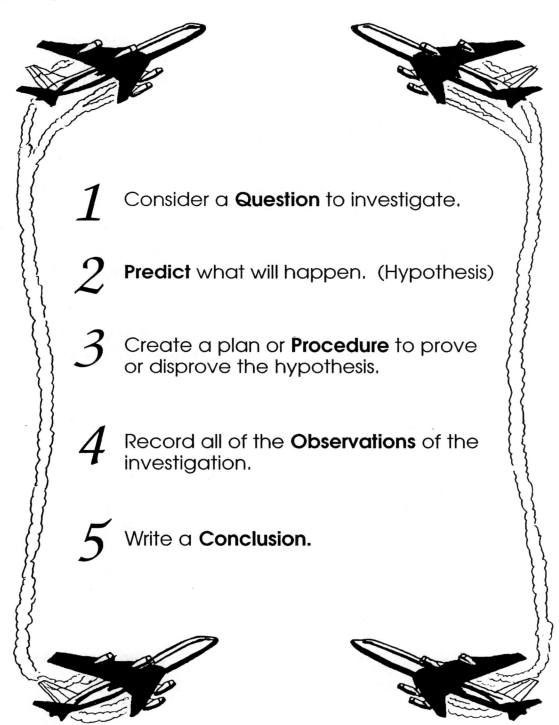

1 Consider a **Question** to investigate.

2 **Predict** what will happen. (Hypothesis)

3 Create a plan or **Procedure** to prove or disprove the hypothesis.

4 Record all of the **Observations** of the investigation.

5 Write a **Conclusion.**

Aviation Timeline

300 B.C. The Chinese constructed kites which were able to stay aloft by floating (gliding) on the breeze.

200 B.C. Archimedes discovered the principle of buoyancy. This principle was used later in the flight of hot air balloons.

1500 There were few accomplishments made until Leonardo da Vinci designed flying machines called ornithopters. The ornithopter required the flapping of its wings.

1903 Orville and Wilbur Wright made a 37 metre (120-foot), 12-second flight at Kitty Hawk, North Carolina. This was the first powered flight in a heavier-than-air machine.

1914 The first airline service began in Florida. The St. Petersburg-Tampa Air Boat Service carried passengers between Tampa and St. Petersburg.

1914 The airplane became a very important part of World War 1. Its successful involvement in the war created the necessity to improve upon the design and production efforts.

1917 The first airmail airline service was launched. The flight began in New York and ended in Philadelphia.

1927 Charles Lindbergh flew the first flight across the Atlantic Ocean from New York to Paris. This was extremely important because it was the first continent-to-continent flight.

1935 Amelia Earhart flew solo across the Pacific Ocean.

1947 The sound barrier was broken by Chuck Yeager.

1986 The first around-the-world flight was made without stopping for fuel. The pilots were Dick Rutan and Jeana Yeager.

Properties of Air

Experiment #1

Question: Does air take up space?

Materials Required:
- one clear glass or jar
- one sheet of paper towel or tissue
- one pail or large bowl
- water

Procedures:
1. Divide the class into groups of 2-3 students.

2. Give each group the materials listed above.

3. Fill the pail with water. (2/3 full)

4. Crumple the paper towel and place it in the bottom of the glass.

5. Turn the glass upside down and submerge it in the water. Make sure that the entire glass is under water.

6. Lift the glass out of the water, making sure not to turn the glass upright.

7. Remove the paper towel from the glass.

8. Observe what happened to the paper towel.

9. Record the results.

Conclusion: The paper towel remained dry because air took up space and prevented the water from entering the glass. Have the students complete the student experiment sheet. Include a diagram.

Properties of Air

Experiment #1 *(con't)*

Question: Does air take up space?

Prediction: _____

_____

_____

Procedures: _____

_____

_____

Observations: _____

_____

_____

_____

_____

Conclusion: _____

_____

_____

_____

_____

Properties of Air

Experiment #1 Diagram

Properties of Air

Experiment #2

Question: Does air expand when heated?

Materials Required:
- one plastic bottle
- one balloon
- one large bowl
- a tea kettle
- water

Procedures:
1. Divide the class into groups of 2-3 students.

2. Give each group the materials listed above.

3. Stretch the balloon over the neck of the bottle.

4. Heat the water and pour it into the bowl.

5. Place and hold the bottle in the bowl.

6. Observe what happens to the balloon.

7. Record the results.

Conclusion: As the air molecules inside the balloon begin to get warmer, they expand. This causes the balloon to expand. Air does expand when heated. Have the students complete the experiment sheet. Include a diagram.

Properties of Air

Experiment #2 *(con't)*

Stretch the balloon over the neck of the bottle.

Stand the bottle in the hot water.

Properties of Air

Experiment #2 (con't)

Question: Does air expand when heated?

Prediction: _____

_____

_____

Procedures: _____

_____

_____

Observations: _____

_____

_____

_____

_____

_____

Conclusion: _____

_____

_____

_____

Properties of Air

Experiment #2 Diagram

Properties of Air

Air Pressure - Activity # 1

Hot

Cool

The purpose of this activity is to demonstrate that air exerts pressure.

Procedure:

1. Pour one cup of boiling water into a plastic bottle and screw the cap on tightly.
2. Allow the contents of the bottle to cool. This may take several minutes.
3. Observe what happens to the bottle.

Results:

1. When the hot water is poured into the bottle, the air pressure (both inside and outside) is equal.
2. When the cap is applied and the bottle is sealed, the air pressure decreases inside the bottle as it cools.
3. Because the air pressure inside is less than the air pressure outside, the air outside begins to push the sides of the bottle inward.

Properties of Air

Activity # 1 Worksheet

Hot   **Cool**

Observations: _____

_____

_____

_____

Why did the sides of the bottle move inward?_____

_____

_____

_____

Properties of Air

Air Pressure - Activity # 2

The purpose of this activity is to demonstrate that air exerts pressure.

Procedure:

1. Place a straw into a plastic bottle and seal the neck of the bottle with tape. This will not allow air to enter or leave the bottle, except through the straw.
2. Place your mouth over the straw and begin drawing the air from the bottle.
3. Continue until you are no longer able to draw out air.
4. Observe the bottle.

Results:

1. The sides of the bottle begin to move inward because the air pressure outside the bottle is much greater than the air pressure inside the bottle.

Properties of Air

Activity # 2 Worksheet

Before	**After**

Observations: _____

_____

_____

_____

Why did the sides of the bottle move inward? _____

_____

_____

_____

Properties of Air

Air Pressure - Activity # 3

The purpose of this activity is to demonstrate that air exerts pressure.

Procedure:

1. Place two straws into your mouth.

2. Put one of the straws into a bottle of water and leave the other straw outside of the bottle.

3. Try to draw water from the bottle into your mouth.

Results:

1. Water cannot be drawn up the straw because equal air pressure has been created in your mouth.

2. If only one straw is used, the air pressure is not equal and water can therefore be drawn into your mouth.

Properties of Air

Activity # 3 Worksheet

Observations: _____

_____

_____

_____

Why could water not be drawn from the bottle? _____

_____

_____

_____

Parts of a Plane

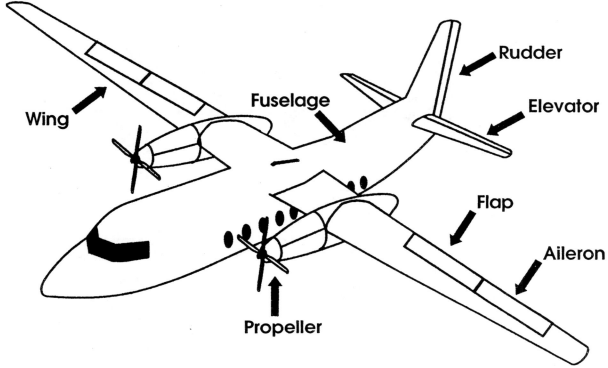

Ailerons - These are small surfaces located at the ends of the wings. If they are angled in opposite directions to each other (i.e. the left aileron is lowered and the right aileron is raised), the plane will roll in the direction of the raised aileron.

Elevator -The elevator can be controlled in an up and down motion. When angled up, the nose of the plane rises and when the elevator is lowered, the nose drops.

Flaps - Flaps are surfaces on the wings which can be raised or lowered to create additional lift or drag. They are used mainly during landing and takeoff.

Fuselage - The fuselage is the main body of the airplane. It can be used to carry cargo or passengers.

Propeller - The propeller creates the forward thrust to increase lift.

Rudder - The rudder is a flap which can be moved right or left. The nose of the plane will move in the direction of the turned rudder.

Wing - The wings permit lift to occur. This allows the plane to fly.

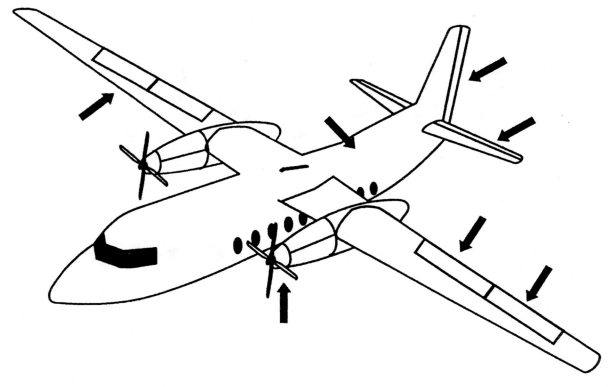

Propeller   Flap   Wing   Fuselage   Aileron   Elevator   Rudder

Ailerons - _____
_____

Elevator - _____
_____

Flaps - _____
_____

Fuselage - _____
_____

Propeller - _____
_____

Rudder - _____
_____

Wing - _____
_____

Characteristics of Flight

Parts of a Plane

Label the parts of a plane using the words below.

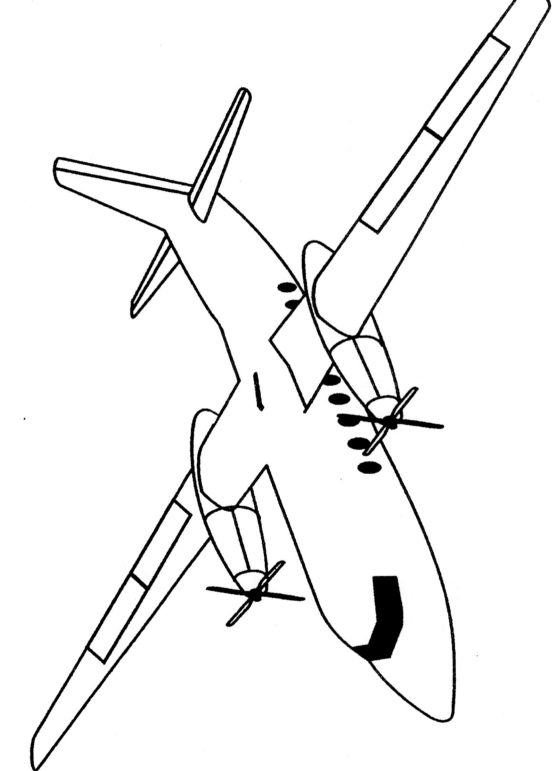

Propeller   Flap   Wing   Fuselage   Aileron   Elevator   Rudder

Parts of a Plane

Nose Art - Activity # 1

It is common for pilots or airline companies to personalize their planes with art designs. Create your own unique design on the airplane's nose.

How Planes Fly

How can something as large and heavy as a plane fly in the air?

There are four main forces which act on a plane. A **force** is a push or a pull on something. You use force when you throw a ball, pull an object or run a race. Forces work in pairs that pull in opposite directions at the same time.

Lift pushes upward, allowing a plane to fly. The **weight** of the airplane pulls in a downward direction. **Thrust** is the force that propels the plane forward. The force that slows an airplane is called **drag**.

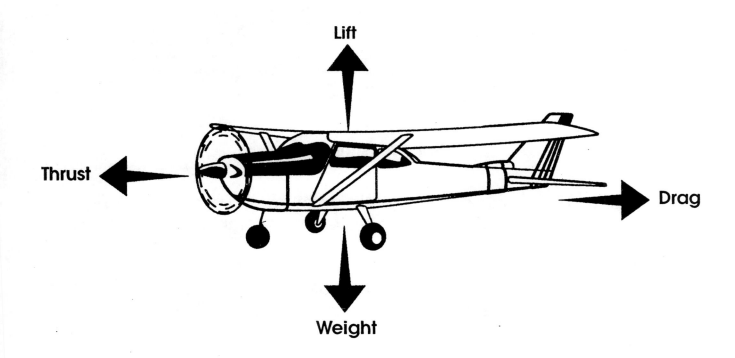

B1-101

How Planes Fly

Forces

Lift occurs as a result of the shape of an airplane's wing. The top, or front of the wing is more curved than the bottom of the wing. The air that flows over the top of the wing moves at a faster speed than the air that flows under the wing. The faster moving air exerts less **pressure** or force than the slower moving air. Therefore, the force under the wing, pulling down (**weight**) is less than the force pulling up (**lift**). **Lift** holds an airplane up.

Thrust (Airplane moving) ➡

Faster Air
(Low Pressure)

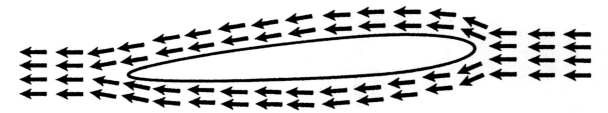

Slower Air
(High Pressure)

Weight is the force which pulls an airplane in a downward direction. **Weight** occurs because of gravity. **Lift** must be greater than **weight** for the plane to rise into the air.

Thrust is the force which moves the plane forward. **Thrust** can be produced by a propeller which pulls the plane forward or by jet exhaust which pushes the plane forward.

Drag is the force which slows the plane down. As the plane moves forward, it meets with resistence from the air and wind.

Activity # 1

This activity will demonstrate how increased air speed over an airplane wing creates **lift**.

1. Cut a strip of paper approximately 25 centimetres (10 inches) long and 5 centimetres (2 inches) wide.

2. Place the end of the paper against your chin just below your bottom lip and let the paper hang without support.

3. Blow air across the paper and observe what happens.

4. Change the air speed by blowing harder and softer. Observe what happens.

5. Record your findings in both words and pictures on the activity sheet provided.

How Planes Fly

Activity # 1 Worksheet

Fast Air	**Slow Air**

Observations: _____

_____

_____

_____

Why did the paper rise? _____

_____

_____

_____

The Glider

A glider is an aircraft that looks much like a plane, but has no engine. Gliders are sometimes referred to as sailplanes. To assist the glider to fly, an airplane tows it into the air. The glider pilot releases the tow line when he/she has reached the desired altitude. In order to attain the speed needed to stay aloft, the glider always must have its nose slightly down. Updrafts can allow the glider to gain altitude and stay up longer. Most flights take about one to five hours in time.

Parts of a Glider

Wings:

The glider's wings are narrower than those of an airplane. This reduces drag. A glider made for competition has wings 22 metres (70 ft) long and 70 centimetres (2.3 ft) wide. A glider flown for recreation has wings of 13 metres (40 ft) by 130 centimetres (4 ft). The lift is produced in the same way as with an airplane.

Body:

The body is the section which extends from the nose to the tail. Many gliders have a canopy so that the pilot can sit up to see. In some competitive gliders, the pilot must lie down to fly the plane, because there is no canopy. The body of the glider is made out of aluminum, fiberglass or wood. The landing gear of the glider is folded up into the body after takeoff.

Tail Assembly:

Often called the empennage, the tail assembly consists of the horizontal stabilizer and elevator, and the vertical fin and rudder.

Type of Planes

Constructing Your Glider

Materials required:

1. glider template
2. scissors
3. styrofoam plate or tray
4. pencil or marker
5. paperclip
6. crayons, pencil crayons or markers

* The glider template is a guide to cut the wings, fuselage and elevator from the styrofoam plate or tray. Assemble the glider by inserting the wings and elevator into the fuselage slots provided.

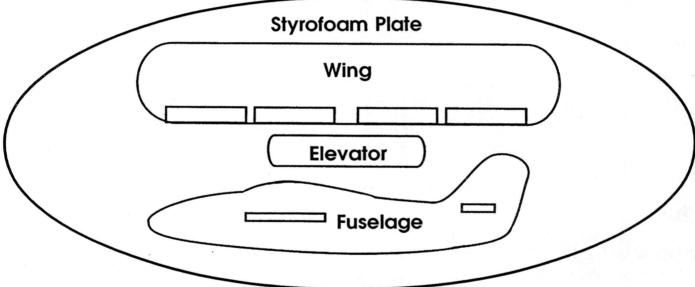

Procedures:

1. Cut out the wing, elevator and fuselage from the glider template.
2. Place the parts of the glider on the styrofoam plate and trace them with a pencil or marker.
3. Cut out the parts of the glider from the styrofoam plate.
4. Decorate the glider parts using crayons, pencil crayons or markers. Do not apply stickers.
5. Assemble the parts of the glider. Trim to fit.
6. Place a paperclip on the nose of the fuselage.
7. Begin flying!

Type of Planes

Glider Template

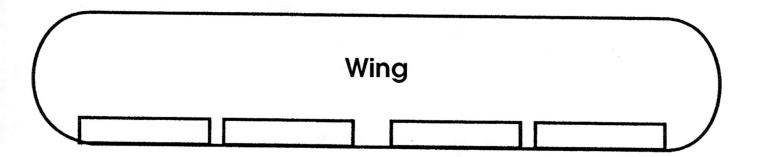

Wing

Elevator

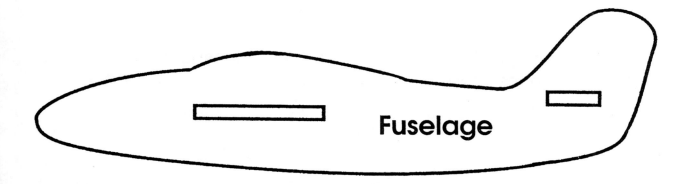

Fuselage

B1-101

Type of Planes

Harrier - Jump Jet

The Harrier is called a VTOL plane which stands for Vertical Takeoff and Landing. It was developed by Britain and the United States. It was one of the first fixed-wing aircraft able to take off and land like a helicopter. The VTOL can hover, takeoff and land vertically, and travel forwards at great speeds. This makes the Harrier ideal for aircraft carriers as it does not require a long runway.

Parts of a Harrier

Exhaust Nozzles:

The Harrier has a unique design feature. The exhaust nozzles from the engine are able to swivel. When the plane is landing or taking off vertically, they are pointed down at the ground. This downward force creates the thrust needed for taking off and landing safely. When the plane reaches its desired altitude, the nozzles are rotated to point backward which, in turn, powers the plane forward.

Wingtip Wheels:

Wingtip wheels are a unique feature of the Harrier jet. The wheels balance the aircraft when it is on the ground and fold up into the wing when the plane is in the air.

Engine:

The Harrier is powered by a single turbofan jet engine. Its top speed at sea level is 1 170 km/h (727 mph).

Type of Planes

Harrier - Jump Jet

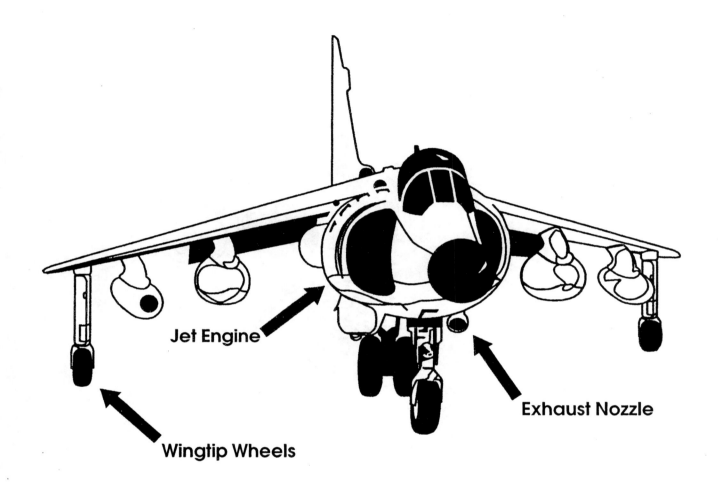

Jet Engine

Wingtip Wheels

Exhaust Nozzle

Type of Planes

Harrier - Jump Jet

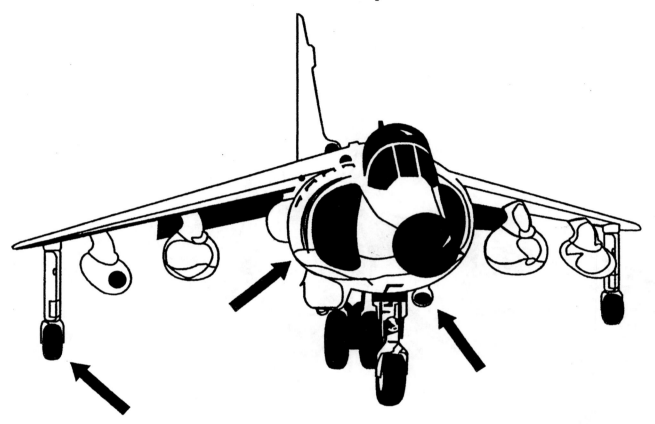

Exhaust Nozzle - _____
_____
_____
_____

Wingtip Wheels - _____
_____
_____

Jet Engine - _____
_____
_____
_____

Type of Planes

The Helicopter

Most planes can only travel forward. The helicopter is able to fly forward, backward and straight up and down. It also has the ability to hover in one place for extended periods of time. The helicopter is able to do this because its overhead blades act as propellers, producing lift and thrust at the same time.

Parts of a Helicopter

Rotor Head:

The rotor head provides the lift and thrust necessary to fly the helicopter. Movable control rods change the angle or pitch of the rotor blades. The rotor head is driven by the engine.

Rotor Blades:

The rotor blades are similar to the wings of an airplane. They are long, narrow blades over which air passes. The difference in air pressure above and below the blade creates lift. The angle of the blades determines whether the helicopter travels forward or backward.

Tail Rotor:

The tail rotor, also made of blades, stabilizes the main body of the helicopter and acts like a rudder for steering.

 B1-101

The Helicopter

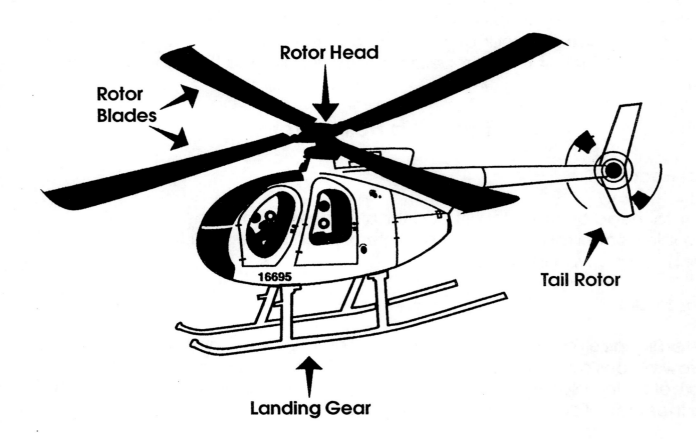

Rotor Head

Rotor Blades

Tail Rotor

16695

Landing Gear

The Helicopter

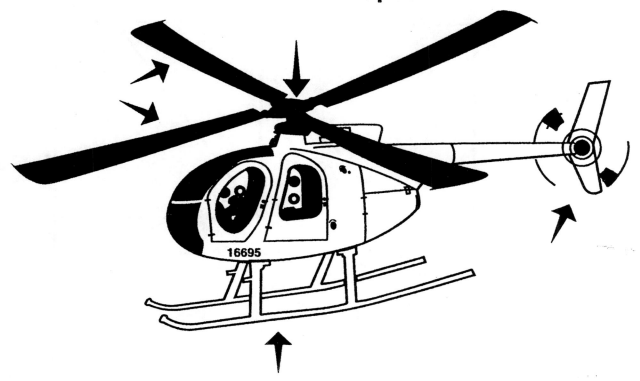

Rotor Head - _____
_____
_____
_____

Rotor Blades - _____
_____
_____
_____

Tail Rotor - _____
_____
_____
_____

Landing Gear - _____
_____
_____

Type of Planes

Helicopter Rotors - Student Activity

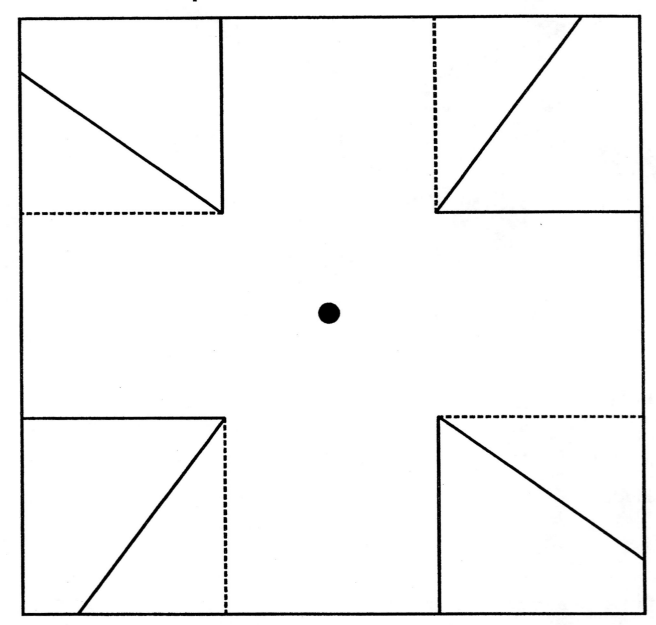

Copy this template onto a piece of cardboard. Cut along solid lines and fold down along dotted lines. Punch a small hole through the middle and place a straw through the hole. Tape the straw firmly in place. Insert a small stick inside the straw and hold the helicopter rotor blades in front of an electric fan. Watch it fly!!

Wordsearch Planes

```
M X L B S S H V I L S A T
E C O I E P E G A A T I M
S O C P A I R L I N E R W
S N K L P T C I R C A S R
E C H A L F U D P A L H G
R O E N A I L E L S T I I
S R E E N R E R A T H P L
C D D F E E S C N E H Y P
H E L I C O P T E R J H I
M H A R R I E R B L I M P
I J U N K E R S W O F Z E
T R I P L A N E F P Q Q R
T O R N A D O Y R L A Q Y
```

airliner	airplane	airship	biplane
blimp	concorde	glider	harrier
helicopter	hercules	junkers	lancaster
lockheed	messerschmitt	piper	seaplane
spitfire	stealth	tornado	triplane

Paper Airplanes

Flying Hints and Ideas

1. Ensure that you fold your paper on a **hard, flat surface**.

2. Copy multiple sheets of each template and **experiment** with different designs.

3. **Design** your own paper airplane and share your results with your classmates.

4. **Colour and decorate** your airplanes. **Do not use stickers.**

5. Airplanes traditionally have **identifying features;** such as registration numbers, pilot's name, company logo or emblem. Include this information when colouring.

6. Experiment with the **positions of the rear flaps**. (i.e. up or down) What happens?

7. Experiment by cutting similar **flaps in the wings**. (i.e. stabilizer) What happens?

8. The **best place to launch** your plane is in a large area, usually indoors.

9. **Test your planes** inside and outside. Where do they perform best?

10. If possible, launch your plane from an **elevated area**. This will allow for **more hang time.**

Paper Airplanes

Airplane #1

Complete Steps 1-8:

1. Cut along the solid lines.
2. Place the paper on a hard flat surface.
3. Fold the paper in half along the centre ① line.
4. Make an inward fold along line ②.
5. Repeat the same fold along line ③ .
6. Fold outwardly along line ④.
7. Place a small piece of tape in the centre and press together.
8. Cut along line ⑤ and fold up or down to achieve the best flight results.

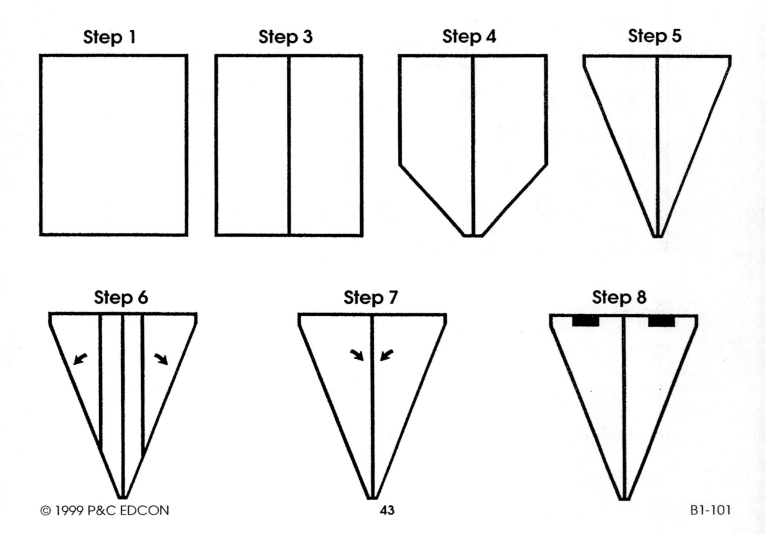

Paper Airplanes

Template #1

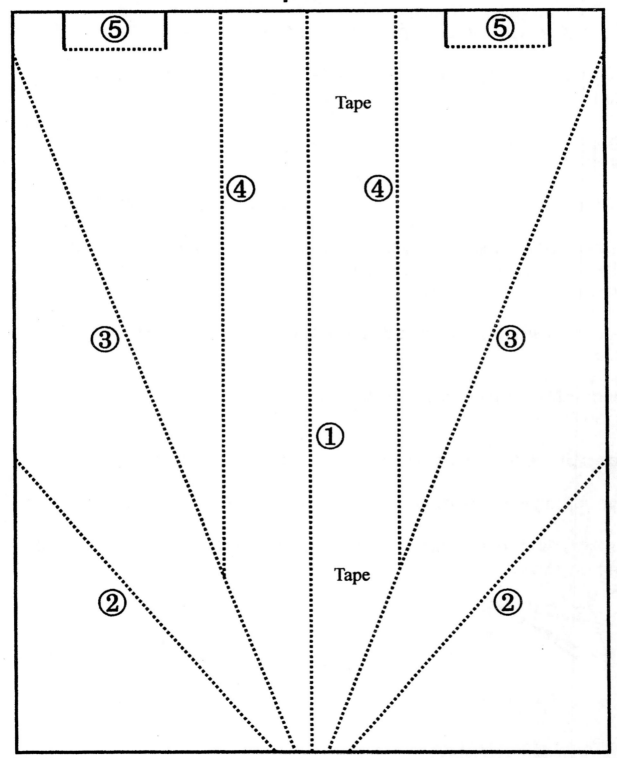

B1-101

Paper Airplanes

Airplane #2

Complete Steps 1-8:

1. Cut along the solid lines.
2. Place the paper on a hard flat surface.
3. Fold the paper in half along the centre ① line.
4. Make an inward fold along line ②.
5. Repeat the same fold along line ③ .
6. Fold outwardly along line ④.
7. Place a small piece of tape in the centre and press together.
8. Cut along line ⑤ and fold up or down to achieve the best flight results.

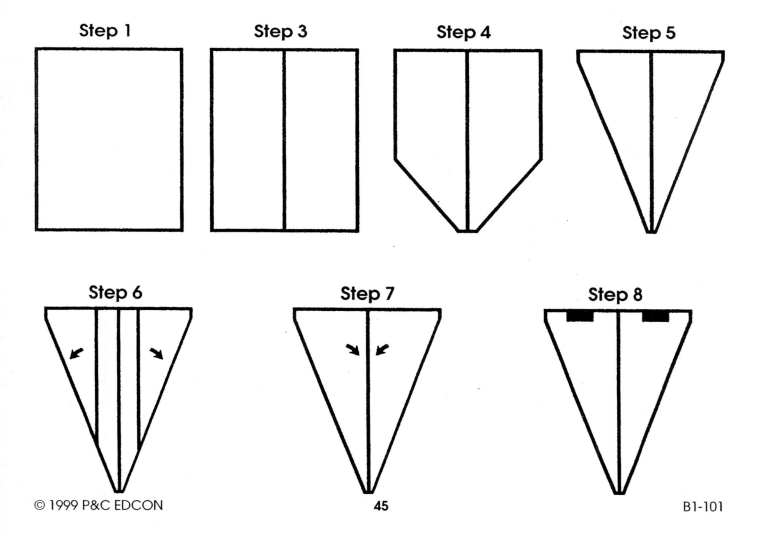

Paper Airplanes

Template #2

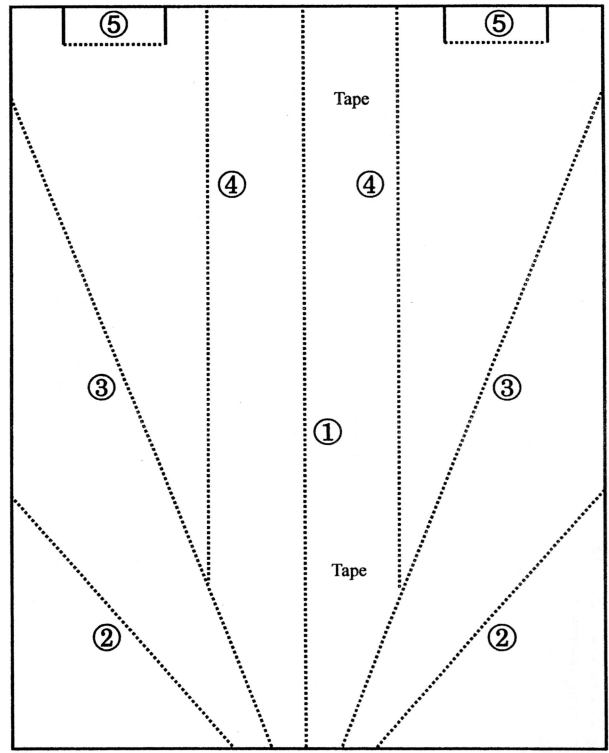

Tape

④ ④

③ ③

①

Tape

② ②

B1-101

Paper Airplanes

Airplane #3

Complete Steps 1-8:

1. Cut along the solid lines.
2. Place the paper on a hard flat surface.
3. Fold the paper in half along the centre ① line.
4. Make an inward fold along line ②.
5. Repeat the same fold along line ③ .
6. Fold outwardly along line ④.
7. Place a small piece of tape in the centre and press together.
8. Cut along line ⑤ and fold up or down to achieve the best flight results.

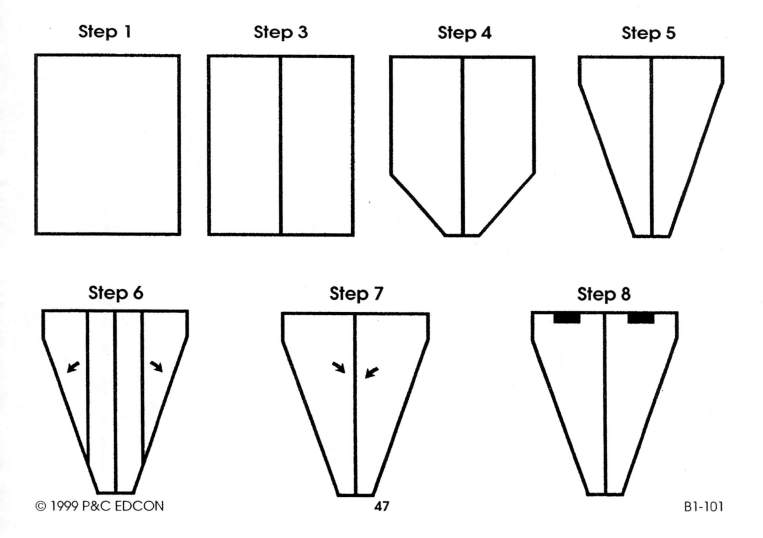

Paper Airplanes

Template #3

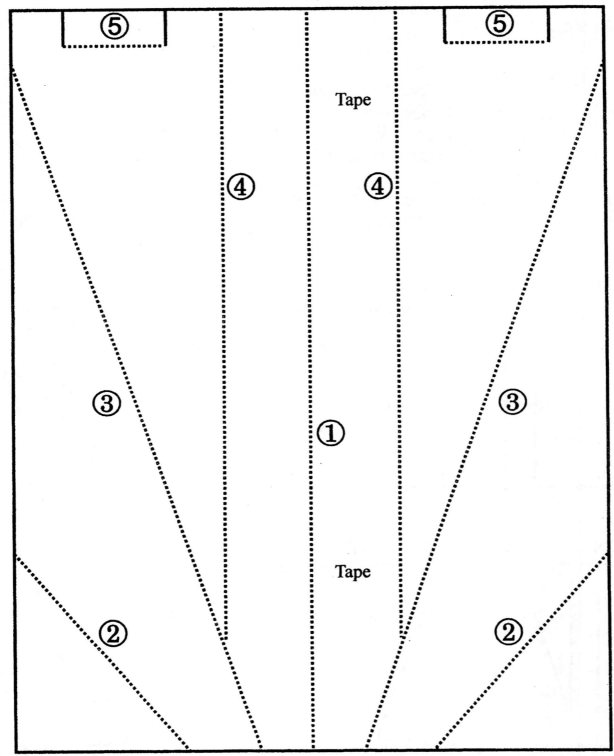

⑤ ⑤

Tape

④ ④

③ ③

①

Tape

② ②

B1-101

Paper Airplanes

Airplane #4

Complete Steps 1-8:

1. Cut along the solid lines.
2. Place the paper on a hard flat surface.
3. Fold the paper in half along the centre ① line.
4. Make an inward fold along line ②.
5. Repeat the same fold along line ③ .
6. Fold outwardly along line ④.
7. Place a small piece of tape in the centre and press together.
8. Cut along line ⑤ and fold up or down to achieve the best flight results.

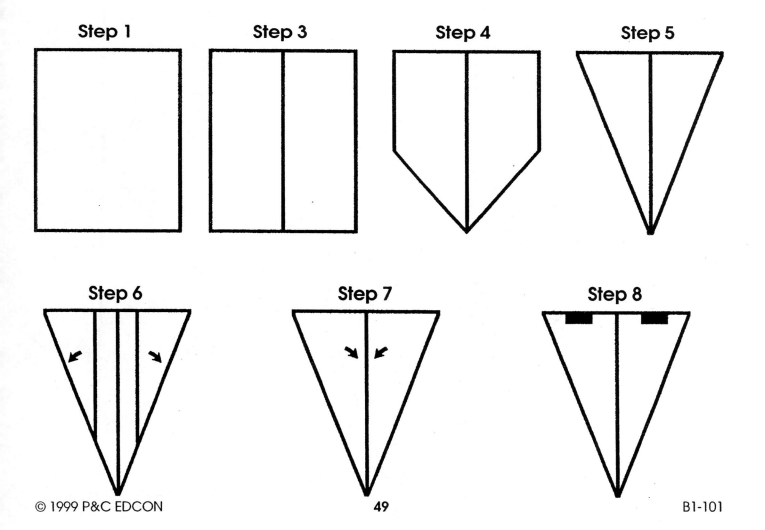

Template #4

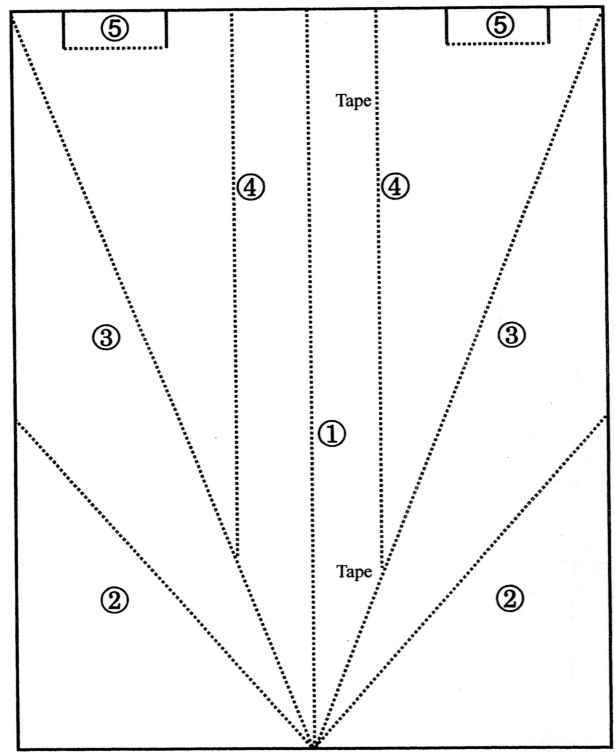

⑤ ⑤

Tape

④ ④

③ ③

①

Tape

② ②

Paper Airplanes

Design your own Paper Airplane
Template #5

B1-101

Paper Airplanes

Experiment #1

Question: **Which paper airplane design flies best?**

Materials Required:
- paper airplane templates/blank paper
- tape (cellulose)
- a tape measure
- a stop watch

Procedures:
1. Give students a copy of each plane template.

2. Ask students to create each plane.

3. Identify each created plane as Design #1, #2, etc.

4. Follow the instructions on the student worksheet for launch angle and flap positions.

5. Time the number of seconds that the plane remains in the air.

6. Record the results.

7. Use the tape measure to calculate the distance the plane travels.

8. Record the results.

Conclusion: Answers will vary. It is **extremely important to maintain a control** on the experiment at all times. i.e. if the flaps are adjusted on one design, **they must be adjusted in the same way on all of the designs**. Have the students complete the student experiment sheet. Include a diagram.

Paper Airplanes

Experiment #1 (con't)

Paper Airplanes

Experiment #1 *(con't)*

Question: Which paper airplane design flies best?

Prediction: _____

_____

_____

Procedures: _____

_____

_____

Observations: _____

_____

_____

_____

_____

_____

Conclusion: _____

_____

_____

_____

_____

Characteristics of Flight

Paper Airplanes

Experiment #1 Worksheet

			Paper Airplane Design #1						
	Flight #1	Flight #2	Flight #3	Flight #4	Flight #5	Flight #6	Flight #7	Flight #8	Flight #9
Angle of Launch	level ✓ up down	level ✓ up down	level ✓ up down	level up ✓ down	level up ✓ down	level up ✓ down	level up down ✓	level up down ✓	level up down ✓
Position of Flaps	level ✓ up down	level up ✓ down	level up down ✓	level ✓ up down	level up ✓ down	level up down ✓	level ✓ up down	level up ✓ down	level up down ✓
Time in Seconds	Results	Results	Results	Results	Results	Results	Results	Results	Results
Length of Flight	Results	Results	Results	Results	Results	Results	Results	Results	Results

B1-101

Paper Airplanes

Experiment #1 Worksheet

Paper Airplane Design #2									
	Flight #1	Flight #2	Flight #3	Flight #4	Flight #5	Flight #6	Flight #7	Flight #8	Flight #9
Angle of Launch	level ✓ up down	level ✓ up down	level ✓ up down	level up ✓ down	level up ✓ down	level up ✓ down	level up down ✓	level up down ✓	level up down ✓
Position of Flaps	level ✓ up down	level up ✓ down	level up down ✓	level ✓ up down	level up ✓ down	level up down ✓	level ✓ up down	level up ✓ down	level up down ✓
Time in Seconds	Results	Results	Results	Results	Results	Results	Results	Results	Results
Length of Flight	Results	Results	Results	Results	Results	Results	Results	Results	Results

Paper Airplanes

Experiment #1 Worksheet

	Flight #1	Flight #2	Flight #3	Flight #4	Flight #5	Flight #6	Flight #7	Flight #8	Flight #9
Paper Airplane Design #3									
Angle of Launch	level ✓ up down	level ✓ up down	level ✓ up down	level up ✓ down	level up ✓ down	level up ✓ down	level up down ✓	level up down ✓	level up down ✓
Position of Flaps	level ✓ up down	level up ✓ down	level up down ✓	level ✓ up down	level up ✓ down	level up down ✓	level ✓ up down	level up ✓ down	level up down ✓
Time in Seconds	Results	Results	Results	Results	Results	Results	Results	Results	Results
Length of Flight	Results	Results	Results	Results	Results	Results	Results	Results	Results

Paper Airplanes

Experiment #1 Worksheet

Paper Airplane Design #4									
	Flight #1	**Flight #2**	**Flight #3**	**Flight #4**	**Flight #5**	**Flight #6**	**Flight #7**	**Flight #8**	**Flight #9**
Angle of Launch	level ✓ up down	level ✓ up down	level ✓ up down	level up ✓ down	level up ✓ down	level up ✓ down	level up down ✓	level up down ✓	level up down ✓
Position of Flaps	level ✓ up down	level up ✓ down	level up down ✓	level ✓ up down	level up ✓ down	level up down ✓	level ✓ up down	level up ✓ down	level up down ✓
Time in Seconds	Results	Results	Results	Results	Results	Results	Results	Results	Results
Length of Flight	Results	Results	Results	Results	Results	Results	Results	Results	Results

Paper Airplanes

Experiment #1 Worksheet

		Flight #1	Flight #2	Flight #3	Flight #4	Flight #5	Flight #6	Flight #7	Flight #8	Flight #9
Paper Airplane Design #5										
Angle of Launch		level ✓ up down	level ✓ up down	level ✓ up down	level up ✓ down	level up ✓ down	level up ✓ down	level up down ✓	level up down ✓	level up down ✓
Position of Flaps		level ✓ up down	level up ✓ down	level up down ✓	level ✓ up down	level up ✓ down	level up down ✓	level ✓ up down	level up ✓ down	level up down ✓
Time in Seconds		Results	Results	Results	Results	Results	Results	Results	Results	Results
Length of Flight		Results	Results	Results	Results	Results	Results	Results	Results	Results

Paper Airplanes

Experiment #1 Graphing

Write a journal entry reporting on your experiment results.

Graph your results.

Paper Airplanes

Experiment #1 Graphing

Using bar graphs, display your results for time and distance.

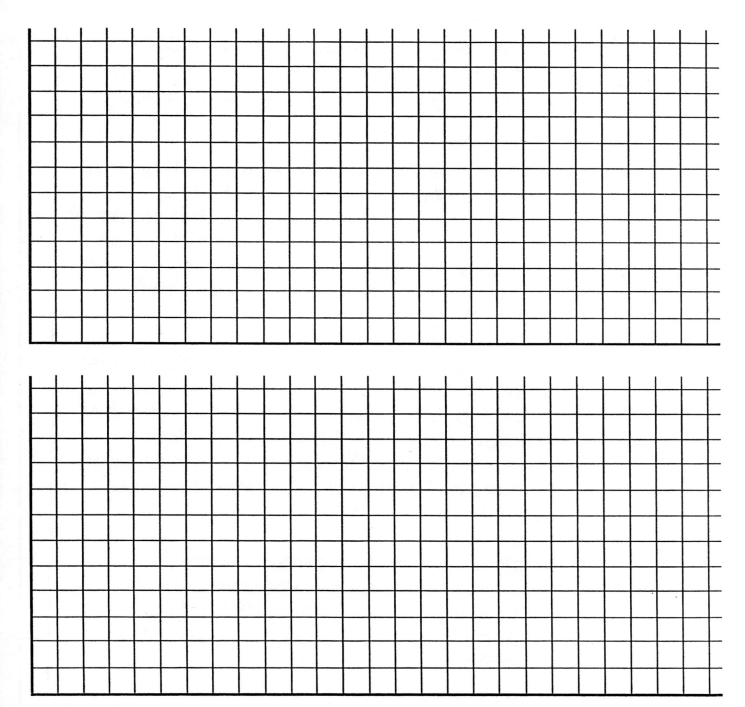

The Wright Brothers

Wilbur Wright was born in 1867 in New Castle, Indiana. His younger brother, Orville, was born in 1871 in Dayton, Ohio. As young men, they went into business together, forming the "Wright Cycle Company" where they made, repaired and sold bicycles.

At this time, many people were experimenting with gliders. This greatly interested the Wright Brothers. They began studying flying. They built gliders, starting in 1899. The Wright Brothers even built a wind tunnel in their shop to help them learn how wings would react to wind. Their desire to create a flying machine grew and grew. Their hard work and hours of study eventually paid off.

Orville and Wilbur chose Kitty Hawk, North Carolina, for their first attempt at flying. On December 17, 1903, their power flying machine took off for the first time. The brothers actually had four flights that day. Orville went first flying 120 feet or 36.5 metres in 12 seconds. Wilbur managed the longest flight, 852 feet or 259.7 metres in 59 seconds. The plane attained a speed of 6.8 miles per hour (10.9 Km/h).

The Wright Brothers continued to improve their flying machine. After two years, the airplane was able to fly 24 miles (38.6 km) in just over 38 minutes. By 1909 the Wright Company was building airplanes. Orville and Wilbur were truly pioneers of aviation.

The Wright Brothers - Activity #1

The Wright Brothers devoted their lives to inventing and improving their flying machine. Their efforts have made life easier for us today.

Research the inventor of a machine that makes your life easier and write a short biography about him or her.

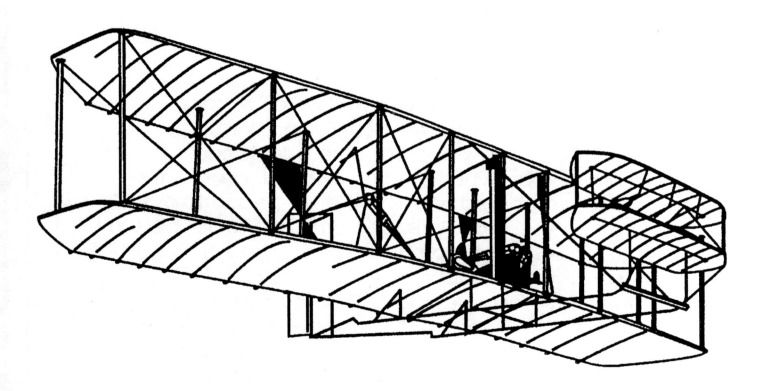

Charles Lindbergh

Charles Lindbergh was born on February 4, 1902. He grew up on a farm near Little Falls, Minnesota. He began studying engineering at the University of Wisconsin when he was 18. He had been interested in flying for a long time. After two years he dropped out of university to attend a school of aviation. Lindberg became a "barnstormer". He and other young fliers travelled around the country, performing flying stunts at exhibitions. Lindbergh's nickname was "Daredevil Lindbergh".

He decided to join the Army so that he could receive better training and learn more about flying. Lindbergh graduated first in his class and became a lieutenant. He flew the first mail plane between St. Louis and Chicago for the army. Lindberg dreamed of being the first person to ever fly nonstop from New York to Paris. The prize for the first person to do this was $25,000. A customized plane, called "The Spirit of St. Louis" was built for Lindbergh, and on May 20, 1927, he took off from New York. He had no parachute because of the added weight. He brought a rubber raft, pocket knife, matches, flares, army rations and just enough drinking water for the trip. To keep himself awake, Lindbergh sang songs and stamped his feet. After more than thirty-three hours and 3,600 miles, "The Spirit of St. Louis" landed safely at an airfield near Paris. For this accomplishment, Lindbergh received the Congressional Medal of Honor and the Distinguished Flying Cross. Charles Lindbergh, an aviation pioneer, died on August 26, 1974.

Charles Lindbergh - Activity #1

Imagine you are Charles Lindbergh. Write a journal entry, dated May 19, 1927 describing your feelings and fears just before you take off.

_____

_____

_____

_____

_____

_____

_____

_____

_____

_____

_____

_____

_____

Charles Lindbergh - Activity #2

Can you unscramble these letters to find words from the Lindberg Story? Use the circled letters to unscramble the bonus word.

ainotaiv

_ _ _ _ _ O _ _

ccaomplhsimnet

OO _ _ _ _ _ _ _ _ O _

snioart

O _ _ _ _ O

eradedivl

_ O _ _ _ _ _ _

zeirp

_ _ _ _ _

ylfeas

_ O _ O _

gnmirotsrnab

_ _ O O _ O _ _ _

uhcteaarp

_ _ _ _ _ _ _ _ _

unstts

_ O _ _ _ _

Bonus Word

OOOOOOOOOOOOO

_____

Famous Aviators

Amelia Earhart

Amelia was born in 1897. During the first World War, she worked as a nurse and became interested in flying through meeting pilots from the Royal Corps. Several years after the war ended, Amelia began flying, making her first solo flight in June, 1921. She loved flying and even had her own airplane.

Amelia caught people's attention when she became the first woman to fly across the Atlantic Ocean. She flew aboard a plane called "Friendship" with two men and was responsible for keeping the log. It bothered Amelia that she was famous for this when she felt she hadn't done anything important. She decided to try to become the first woman to fly alone across the Atlantic Ocean. In May, 1932, she successfully flew a Lockheed Vega monoplane from Newfoundland across the ocean to Ireland in less than fifteen hours. She was a founding member of an organization of women pilots called the "Ninety-Nines".

Amelia went on to set other world records. In 1935, she was the first solo pilot to fly from Hawaii to the mainland. She decided to attempt the first flight around the world. On June 1, 1937, Amelia and her navigator, Frederick Noonan, took off from Miami, Florida. She made it to Lae, New Guinea, but while on route to her next stop on Howland Island, reported a Mayday (emergency). Ships in the area searched for the plane in vain. Emelia Earhart never reached tiny Howland Island and was never seen again.

Amelia Earhart - Activity #1

Some people believe Amelia Earhart is still alive. Others believe she made an emergency landing on an island and was killed by the people there. This mystery has puzzled people for years.

Write your own version of Amelia Earhart's flight around the world. How will your story end?

Famous Aviators

Chuck Yeager

Chuck Yeager was born in 1923. At the age of 18, he enlisted in the Air Force and by 1942 had been commissioned as a flight officer. He flew sixty-four missions during World War II, flying with the eighth Air Force Fighter Command. On his ninth mission, Yeager was shot down by German planes. Though wounded, he was able to escape capture. He received many awards, including the Silver Star, the Distinguished Flying Cross, the Air Medal, the Bronze Star and the Purple Heart, for his achievements during World War II.

When the war ended, Yeager was assigned to Ohio's Wright-Patterson Air Force Base, in the fighter flight test branch. He became the test pilot for the X-1 rocket airplane project. Some of his test flights included glide and partial-powered flights of the X-1. The Air Force thought that Yeager and the X-1 should try to break the sound barrier. No other person had yet been able to do this.

At sea level, sound travels at approximately 763 miles per hour (1228 Km/h). It had taken many years to create a plane able to travel faster than this. On October 14, 1947, Yeager began his attempt. He and the X-1 were carried inside a B-29 bomber plane to an altitude of 26,000 feet (7925 metres). The B-29 dove 1,000 feet (305 metres) and then released the X-1. Yeager started the rocket engines and accelerated until the X-1 passed the speed of sound (known as Mach 1). Two months later, Chuck Yeager and the X-1 again beat the speed of sound, reaching a top speed of 1,650 miles per hour (2655 Km/h).

Chuck Yeager - Activity #1

Write T for true or F for false beside each statement.

_____ Yeager joined the Air force when he was 21 years old.

_____ Yeager flew 64 missions during World War II.

_____ When his plane was shot down, Yeager managed to escape.

_____ After the war, Yeager became an airline pilot.

_____ The X-1 was a rocket airplane.

_____ The sound barrier was broken in 1945.

_____ Sound travels at approximately 500 kph (320 mph).

_____ Yeager and the X-1 were carried inside a B-29 bomber.

_____ Mach 1 is another name for the speed of sound.

_____ Chuck Yeager flew faster than the speed of sound only once.

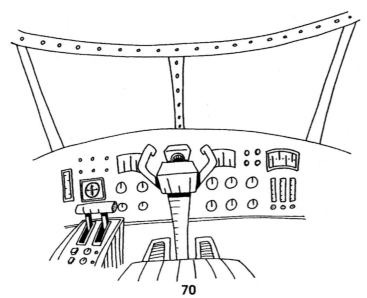

Famous Aviators

Chuck Yeager - Activity #2

You have been asked to create a special award to be presented to Chuck Yeager, in recognition of being the first to break the sound barrier.

Draw a picture of your design and give it a title.

John Gillespie Magee Jr.
1922-1941

John Gillespie Magee, Jr. was born to American parents in Shanghai, China, in 1922. He was 18 years old when he crossed the United States/Canadian border and joined the Royal Canadian Air Force. During his first year, he was sent to England and joined the No. 412 Fighter Squadron, RCAF. He completed his training and flew a Submarine Spitfire.

Magee rose to the rank of Pilot Officer while flying missions over France and England against the German Luftwaffe. It was during this time that the Battle of Britain was fought.

On September 3, 1941, during a high altitude (30,000 feet) test flight, Magee was inspired by his surroundings to write his thoughts in a poem. After returning to the ground, he wrote a letter to his parents. In it he wrote, "I am enclosing a verse I wrote the other day. It started at 30,000 feet, and was finished soon after I landed." In his letter, he included the poem, "High Flight".

On December 11, 1941 Pilot Officer John Gillespie Magee, Jr. was killed. His plane collided with another during training, while flying in the clouds. He was only 19 years old.

High Flight

Oh, I have slipped the surly bonds of earth

And danced the skies on laughter-silvered wings;

Sunward I have climbed and joined the tumbling mirth

Of sun-split clouds – and done a hundred things

You have not dreamed of – wheeled and soared and swung

High in the sunlit silence. Hov'ring there,

I've chased the shouting wind along, and flung

My eager craft through footless halls of air.

Up, up the long, delirious, burning blue

I've topped the windswept heights with easy grace,

Where never lark, or even eagle, flew;

And, while with silent, lifting mind I've trod

The high untrespassed sanctity of space,

Put out my hand and touched the face of God.

By John Gillespe Magee, Jr.
September 3, 1941

B1-101

High Flight

High Flight - Activity #1

In a **Shape Poem**, words are written so that they create an outline of the object or shape described in the poem. Using the flight theme, have each student write his or her own shape poem.

Example:

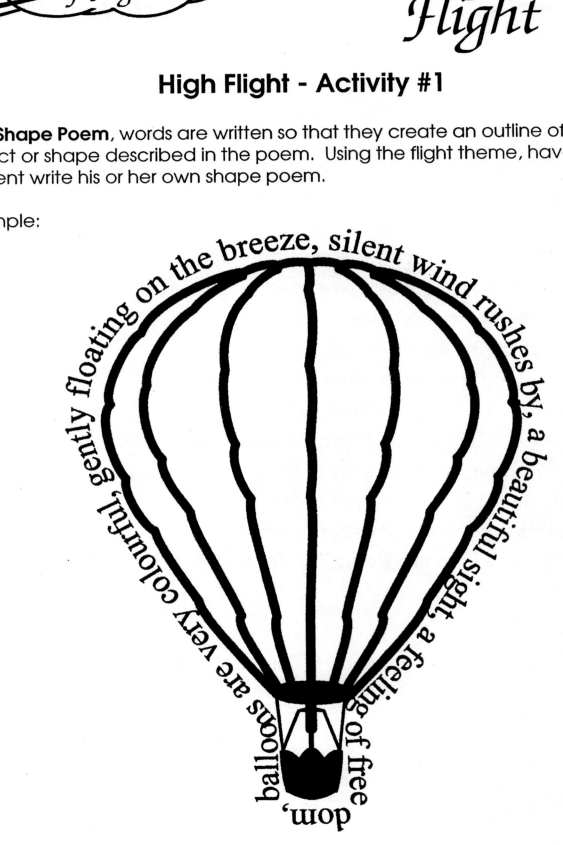

gently floating on the breeze, silent wind rushes by, a beautiful sight, a feeling of free dom, balloons are very colourful,

Invention Conference

Dear Parents,

Your children will soon be participating in an **Invention Conference**. It is designed to promote creative problem-solving and encourage independent thinking skills. They will follow a sequential process to invent a new product or develop a new method of completing a task.

We will begin by discussing existing inventions and, if possible, their inventors. This will allow the children to gain an appreciation for the invention process.

It is necessary to first find an idea for an invention. You may be asked if you have need for a new product or if you require a new method to solve a problem or lessen your workload. Your participation and encouragement will make the children's experience a positive one.

Once an idea has been established, research is necessary to ensure that the idea has not already been invented. An **Invention Declaration** form will be completed and will require your signature. After approval has been given, your son or daughter may begin to plan and compete the invention.

During the actual process of inventing and building, the children may need to be reminded that many inventors have met with failure along the way. **Constant encouragement is needed throughout the process!**

Once the invention has been assembled, a **Patent Application** will need to be completed. **Your interest and encouragement will ensure that this science experience is unforgettable!**

Inventions are required at school on _____

Sincerely,

Invention Conference

Invention Ideas

"I don't know what to do. I can't think of anything."

The following list of invention ideas is to be used to motivate and encourage young inventors.

- a new suitcase design
- a new book bag
- a new container
- a new travel game
- a new parachute design
- a new board game
- a new clothing design
- a new cleaning tool
- a new toy
- a new product for pets

- a method of keeping drinks cold
- a new way of organizing pencils
- a new way to remember things
- a way to prevent spills
- a new paper airplane design
- a new garbage collection method
- a method of cleaning your room
- a new airport design
- a new toothbrush holder
- a new use for household items

Invention Conference

Successful inventions are ones that make improvements to existing products, solve problems or meet a specific need. Make a list of improvements that would help your community, school or home. Use this list to help you to decide on an invention topic

Name: _____

Date: _____

Improvement, problem, need:

_____

_____

_____

Materials required:

_____

_____

_____

Invention description:

_____

_____

_____

_____

_____

_____

_____

_____

_____

Invention Conference

Invention Declaration

Inventor_____
        (Last Name)   *(First Name)*

Address_____

City _____ Province _____

Postal Code _____Telephone (   ) _____

School _____ Teacher _____

Invention Description (brief)

_____
_____
_____

Research Completed

_____
_____
_____

Materials List

_____
_____
_____

Invention Due _____   _____
                                        (Inventor's Signature)

                                  _____
                                        (Parent's Signature)

Invention Conference

Invention Sketch

Complete a diagram of your invention

Invention Conference

Application for a Patent

I, _____, the undersigned, do declare that the information provided below is truthful and accurate. It is my belief that I am the creator of an original invention called:

_____

Declaration

Inventor (Full Name): _____

Address: _____

City: _____ Province:_____

Postal Code: _____ Telephone:_____

School: _____ Grade:_____

Teacher: _____

Principal:_____

I believe that my invention is original and the first of its kind in Canada.

Inventor's Signature:_____ Date:_____

Invention Conference

Invention Conference Evaluation

Inventor: _____ Grade_____

Invention: _____

Originality
```
├────────┼────────┼────────┼────────┤
0        5        10       15       20
```

Design
```
├────────┼────────┼────────┼────────┤
0        5        10       15       20
```

Research
```
├────────┼────────┼────────┼────────┤
0        5        10       15       20
```

Use in Society
```
├────────┼────────┼────────┼────────┤
0        5        10       15       20
```

Production Cost
```
├────┼────┼────┼────┤
0         5         10
```

Presentation
```
├────┼────┼────┼────┤
0         5         10
```

Total Score _____

Judged by _____

B1-101

Characteristics of Flight

Name: _____ **Date:** _____

Future Flight

Planes of the Future

Draw a picture of your plane. Name your plane, explain how it will be used and list some important facts about it.

Collage

Using old magazines, catalogues and newspaper articles, find examples of things that fly. Glue them onto a large piece of construction paper to create a **Characteristics of Flight** collage.

Experiment

Question: _____

_____

Prediction: _____

_____

_____

_____

Procedures: _____

_____

_____

_____

Observations: _____

_____

_____

_____

_____

_____

_____

Conclusion: _____

_____

_____

_____

_____

B1-101

Wordsearch

```
H M V S R F L I G H T E
E I I Q N E T S U R H T
L X X W L O N D R A G F
I R E D D U R I E B S U
C O N C O R D E L T A S
O T B O E I N G L R V E
P A R A C H U T E I I L
T V G O L L W F P P A A
E E G V P L N I O L T G
R L O Y H R O L R A I E
R E D I L G I O P N O V
W A E O T P L A N E N A
```

ailerons	drag	parachute
airliner	elevator	plane
airport	flight	propeller
aviation	fuselage	rudder
balloon	glider	thrust
boeing	helicopter	triplane
concorde	lift	

Brainstorm

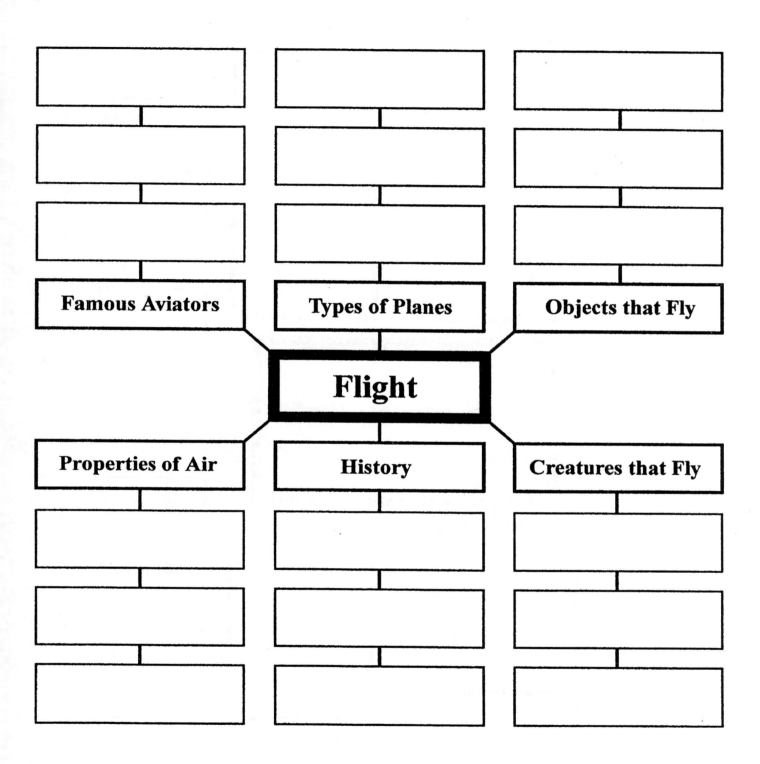

Famous Aviators

Types of Planes

Objects that Fly

Flight

Properties of Air

History

Creatures that Fly

B1-101

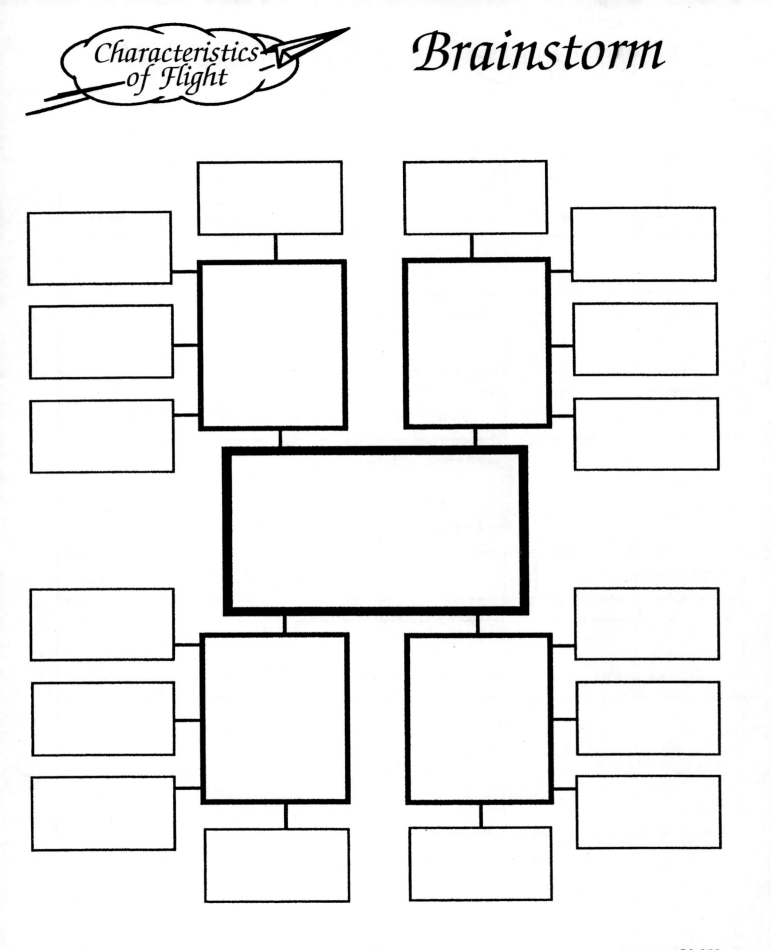

B1-101

Evaluation

Evaluation Key
V - Very Good
G - Good
S - Satisfactory
N - Needs
   Improvement

Students' Names

B1-101

Grouping

Classroom Groups

Conference

Name: _____ **Date:**_____

Activity Title	Rating					Comments
	1 very poor	**2** poor	**3** good	**4** very good	**5** excellent	
	1	2	3	4	5	
	1	2	3	4	5	
	1	2	3	4	5	
	1	2	3	4	5	
	1	2	3	4	5	
	1	2	3	4	5	
	1	2	3	4	5	
	1	2	3	4	5	
	1	2	3	4	5	
	1	2	3	4	5	
	1	2	3	4	5	
	1	2	3	4	5	
	1	2	3	4	5	
	1	2	3	4	5	
	1	2	3	4	5	
	1	2	3	4	5	
	1	2	3	4	5	
	1	2	3	4	5	
	1	2	3	4	5	
	1	2	3	4	5	
	1	2	3	4	5	

Student's Signature _____ **Teacher's Signature:** _____

Excellence in Science Award

Name

has successfully completed the unit on

Characteristics of Flight

Congratulations!

Teacher

Date

FLIGHT

Charles Lindbergh - Activity #2

ainotaiv
a v i a t i o n

ccaomplhsimnet
a c c o m p l i s h m e n t

snioart
r a t i o n s

eradedivl
d a r e d e v i l

zeirp
p r i z e

ylfeas
s a f e l y

gnmirotsrnab
b a r n s t o r m i n g

uhcteaarp
p a r a c h u t e

unstts
s t u n t s

Bonus Word

t r a n s a t l a n t i c

Chuck Yeager - Activity #1

F   Yeager joined the Air force when he was 21 years old.

T   Yeager flew 64 missions during World War II.

T   When his plane was shot down, Yeager managed to escape.

F   After the war, Yeager became an airline pilot.

T   The X-1 was a rocket airplane.

F   The sound barrier was broken in 1945.

F   Sound travels at approximately 500 kph (320 mph).

T   Yeager and the X-1 were carried inside a B-29 bomber.

T   Mach 1 is another name for the speed of sound.

F   Chuck Yeager flew faster than the speed of sound only once.

Characteristics of Flight

Wordsearch Answer Keys

Wordsearch Planes (from page 41)

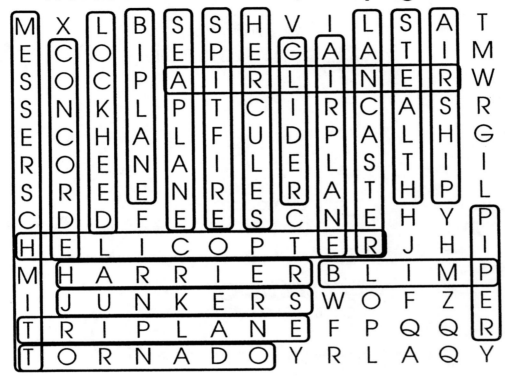

Wordsearch (from page 86)

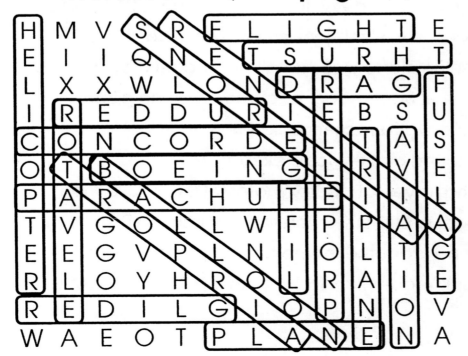

B1-101